Contents

What Is Bullying?

Bullying is not a new problem. Parents, schools, and governments have long wrestled with how to deal with the issue. In our society, where emerging technologies unite us in new ways, bullying is being recognized as an epidemic. Most students can identify and describe bullying behavior, but it is important to move beyond the basics and provide a safe forum in our classrooms to explore the complexity of the bullying web. Activating prior knowledge and prior experience is a place to start; sharing expert opinions, research, and statistics can help us explore our own stories and feelings.

ACTIVITY: CONSIDERING EXPERT VOICES

As you read the words from expert psychologists in the box to the right, what stories are you reminded of from your own life? From the lives of others? Respond in writing or work in small groups to share thoughts on one or all three quotes.

Expert Voices

- Bullying is a relationship problem in which power and aggression are used to cause distress to a vulnerable person.—*Wendie M. Craig and Debra J. Pepler, Professors of Psychology*
- Bullying is when someone does or says something to hurt someone else. It is always on purpose. …Bullying is about making someone feel small and powerless.—*Kids Help Phone*
- Being bullied is…a public health problem. …People who were bullied as children are more likely to suffer depression and low self-esteem well into adulthood, and the bullies themselves are more likely to engage in criminal behavior in later life.—*Duane Alexander, Director for the National Institute of Child Health and Human Development*

Defining the Bully

It is important to consider how bullying is different from other areas of conflict. In defining the concept of *bully*, choose vocabulary you think is relevant and try to articulate the behaviors inherent in bullying situations.

ACTIVITY: BULLY IN THE DICTIONARY

1. You have been assigned the job of defining the word "bully" for a dictionary. Consider the characteristics, behaviors, and intentions of someone who is a bully. Write a definition of 25 words or less.
2. In pairs, combine your definitions. Negotiate ideas and devise a new definition of the word.
3. In groups of four, share definitions to compare similarities and differences. Collaborate to write a definition that is exactly 25 words in length.
4. As a class, collaborate to create a class definition of the word "bully" of 50 words or less.

Extensions

- Investigate definitions of bullying in a dictionary, on the Internet, or in other resources.
- Consider this definition of bullying by Barbara Coloroso:

> Bullying is a conscious, wilful, and deliberate hostile activity intended to harm, induce fear through the threat of further aggression and create terror. (2002: 13)

What words from your definition are similar to Coloroso's? How might you alter her definition?

Let's Talk About…the Media

- What movies or TV shows have you seen about the bullying issue?
- What stories have you read in newspapers or magazines about bullying incidents?
- What novels or picture books have you read about bullies and their victims?

Key Issues

ACTIVITY: ON THE LINE

As a class, form a line for each of these statements. If you strongly agree, move to the left of the line; strongly disagree, to the right. If you mildly agree, stand centre left; mildly disagree, centre right. Give reasons for your choice.

Statement #1: The best way to stop bullying is to stand up to the bully.

Statement #2: Cyberbullying is not a school problem.

Statement #3: All bullying incidents must be reported to an adult.

Statement #4: Not responding to a mean message on Twitter is the best way to deal with it.

Extensions

- It is important to hear everyone's opinions. Have a discussion with others who have different opinions about the issue.
- Repeat the activity with the option of changing positions on the continuum after listening to the arguments of others.

Let's Talk About…Key Issues

- What do you think are the three top reasons why people bully?
- What advice would you give someone with bullying behaviors?
- How can these behaviors be changed?

ACTIVITY: THE BULLY, THE BULLIED, THE BYSTANDER

1. Record your answers to these five prompts on a file card:
   - One word to describe a bully is…
   - One word to describe a target is…
   - An animal I think a bully can be compared to is… Explain your choice.
   - An animal I think a target can be compared to is… Explain your choice.
   - If I saw someone being bullied I would…

2. Work in groups of five or six to share your responses to the prompts. Work as a class to share answers.

Just the Facts

Statistics about bullying are often made available through surveys. The numbers are powerful, and often shocking, indicators of the prevalence of bullying among young people.

ACTIVITY: CONSIDERING STATISTICS

Discuss with a partner which of these statements surprises you most.

- 71% of teachers say they intervene in bullying episodes; 25% of students say teachers intervene. (Pepler & Craig, 2000)
- Each day, more than 160,000 North American students miss school for fear of being bullied. (National Education Association)
- One out of every four kids is abused by another youth. (American Justice Department)
- Even though bystanders don't like to watch bullying, less than 20% try to stop it. (Family Resources Facilitation Program)
- 58% of kids admit someone has said or done something mean to them online; about 50% claim it has happened more than once. (i-Safe America)

ACTIVITY: IS THAT TRUE?

One of these statements is false. Work with a partner and share your reactions to each of these facts.

A. 90% of all cyberbullying incidents go unreported to adults.
B. Bullying occurs once every 7 minutes on the playground and once every 25 minutes in the classroom.
C. Most bullying incidents happen in secondary school.

ACTIVITY: GATHERING FACTS

On the Internet find 5 to 10 recent statistics about bullying and cyberbullying. Prepare a True/False quiz to share with others.

Example: When a friend steps in, bullying stops half of the time in ten seconds.   T   F

Answers

Is That True? C is false. Some of the top years of bullying happen before high school: 90% of 4th- through 8th-graders have been reported as victims of some kind of bullying.
Gathering Facts True

1. UNDERSTANDING BULLYING

Caught in the Web

Cyberbullying is the deliberate use of digital media—e.g., social-networking sites, texting—to inflict harm or to communicate false, embarrassing, or hostile information. It includes

- private e-mails forwarded without consent
- threatening texts
- verbal attacks through social media
- embarrassing photos posted without permission
- video hate lists

It is essential to discuss issues of cyberbullying in the classroom to provide students with strategies for preventing and dealing with online harassment.

ACTIVITY: WHAT IF...?

Review the list in the blue box and choose one situation. In a written response, share your reactions to this *what-if* situation and write about a personal incident or connection this scenario reminds you of. Meet with others who chose the same scenario and discuss possible solutions to the problem.

Extension

Work in pairs or small groups to discuss the What If...? scenarios. As a group, focus on one item or discuss solutions for handling each cyberbullying dilemma.

1. What if...you receive an e-mail message spreading a nasty rumor about one of your best friends?
2. What if...your brother or sister says they received a nasty e-mail and asks you not to tell your parents?
3. What if...you receive mean text messages that, over a month, get worse?
4. What if...some of your friends decide to post a video of a friend doing something stupid online as a joke?
5. What if...you have just read some rude comments on a blog that upset you?
6. What if...you and your best friend get into a fight and later you read mean comments about you on his/her Facebook page?

Dealing with Tragedy

At the extreme end of the bully trap is *bullycide*, young people who choose to kill themselves rather than face one more day of being bullied. The rate of bullying-related suicide attempts has tripled over the past three decades. Particularly heartbreaking are the victims of bullying who post online messages announcing to the world that they have been caught in the endless cycle of bullying. Most targets have been taunted online; even if we are not directly engaged with an incident, we are exposed to this information through social media.

Online In Memoriam

"I'm tired of life, really. It's so hard. I'm sorry. I can't take it anymore."
— Jamie Hubley *November 23, 1995–October 14, 2011*

"I always say how bullied I am but no one listens."
— Jamey Rodemeyer *March 21, 1997–September 18, 2011*

"I have nobody I need someone"
— Amanda Todd *November 10, 1996–October 10, 2012*

Social media can act as a platform for expressing sympathy and paying tribute to those who have died. But the stories of Jamie, Jamey, and Amanda also provoked horrifying hate messages online: "He deserved to die." "She brought it on herself." What do you think makes someone that hateful toward someone they have never met?

Teacher Talk

Do we discuss these sensitive stories in the classroom? How can we not? Reasons for suicide are complex. But it is important to explore the stories of those who scream, "I can't take it anymore!" Are we brave enough to bring these stories into the classroom, with the range of sympathetic, uncomfortable, and guilty responses they arouse? What is the alternative to building empathy?

Let's talk about...Hate

- In groups, discuss: "Why do people hate?"
- Do we condone hate with our silence?

Literacy Approaches to Bullying

In our literacy classrooms, students are encouraged to read, write, and talk. The fiction and information sources can provide contexts for us to share ideas, and to listen and respond to those around us. To confront the bullying issue, we need to deal with tough questions, make connections to personal and world stories, and reach an understanding of why someone behaves as a bully. By reading novels, picture books, poems, newspaper reports, and information in print or online, we can be better prepared to understand how to take action when ongoing, deliberate threats arise.

Teacher Talk

By having a chance (and the trust) to respond independently, in pairs, in small groups, or with the whole class—both out loud and in writing—to bullying-centred stories, students can communicate with, collaborate with, and be compassionate of others. They can come to learn to care.

ACTIVITY: PREPARING AN ANNOTATED BIBLIOGRAPHY

1. Work in a small group to prepare a list of resources you can share with others to help them understand the bullying issue. Lists of titles are on pages 12–13.
2. In an annotated bibliography, information is provided that summarizes the book. You might decide to include a short review and state why someone might be interested in reading it or using it.
3. As a group, discuss how you will organize your resource list; you can use headings, such as the ones provided on pages 12–13 (e.g., Picture Books, Novels, etc.).

Annotated Bibliography Sample

Roy, James (2009) *Max Quigley: Technically Not a Bully* Max Quigley is a bully who plays a trick on one of his 6th-grade classmates, who he thinks is a geek. As it turns out, Max's punishment is to be tutored by the boy he bullied, and along the way he learns about tolerance and acceptance. This novel, with cartoon sketches, was originally published in Australia.

The ABCs of Anti-Bullying

ACTIVITY: THE VOCABULARY OF ANTI-BULLYING

Work with a partner. On a sheet of paper, write the letters *A* to *Z*. For each letter, list one or more words connected to the concept of bullying: feelings, actions, characteristics, or behaviors connected to the bully, the bullied, or a bystander. Share your ABC list with another pair. What words from their list would you like to add to your own?

ACTIVITY: BULLYING ALPHABET BOOK

Working in a group of three or four, prepare an illustrated anti-bullying alphabet for younger students. For example, "*A* is for *Angry*; *B* is for *Bystander*; *C* is for *Compassion*…" You can give information about each term in words and/or through illustration; e.g., drawing, magazine cutouts, photos found online.

ACTIVITY: GLOSSARY OF ANTI-BULLYING

A glossary, like a dictionary, is a list of words with definitions; however, the words in a glossary are usually connected to a theme or topic. Choose 10 to 12 words from your ABC list and prepare a Glossary of Anti-Bullying by giving short explanations for the terms.

Let's Talk About…Books

- What book best captures the world of bullying?
- How do you think a novel or picture book can help someone caught in the bullying trap?
- Do you think humorous stories about bullying incidents are helpful?

Resource List

On pages 12–13 is a list of 90 titles. Picture books are recommended for read-alouds and for students to read independently and engage with. Chapter books and novels are outlined, as well as reference materials that provide information and support for those involved with bullying incidents. Anthologies document authentic stories of bullying and video sources offer significant media to respond to.

Teacher Talk

Encourage students to add to this list and make recommendations to others seeking resources about the bullying topic. Preparing an Annotated Bibliography (on page 10) is one way for students to share information about books.

Top Tens

TEN PICTURE BOOKS FOR THE TEACHER TO READ ALOUD

Bromley, Anne C.; Illus., Robert Casilla, *The Lunch Thief.*

Browne, Anthony, *Willy the Champ.* (Also: *Willy the Wimp, Willy and Hugh*)

Bunting, Eve; Illus. David Frampton, *Riding the Tiger.*

Cannon, Janell, *Crickwing.*

Choi, Yangsook, *The Name Jar.*

Lester, Helen; Illus. Lynn Munsinger, *Hooway for Wodney Wat.*

Mobin-Uddin, Asma; Illus. Barbara Kiwak, *My Name is Bilal.*

Moss, Peggy; Illus. Lea Lyon, *Say Something.*

Polacco, Patricia, *Bully.* (Also: *Mr. Lincoln's Way*)

Sesskin, Steve & Allen Shamblin; Illus. Glin Dibley, *Don't Laugh At Me.*

TEN BOOKS FOR VERY YOUNG READERS

Agassi, Martine, *Hands Are Not for Hitting.*

Alexander, Martha, *I Sure Am Glad to See You, Blackboard Bear.*

Bateman, Teresa; Illus. Jackie Urbanovic, *The Bully Blockers Club.*

Cosby, Bill; Illus. Varnette P. Honeywood, *The Meanest Thing to Say.*

Cox, Phil Roxbee; Illus. Jan McCafferty, *Don't Be A Bully, Billy.*

dePaola, Tomie, *Oliver Button is a Sissy.*

Lalli, Judy, *Make Someone Smile… and 40 more ways to be a peaceful person.*

Mayer, Gina & Mercer, *Just a Bully.*

Thomas, Pat, *Stop Picking on Me: A first look at bullying.*

Verdick, Elizabeth; Illus. Marieka Heinlen, *Words Are Not for Hurting.*

TEN PICTURE BOOKS FOR INDEPENDENT READING

Alexander, Claire, *Lucy and the Bully.*

Casley, Judith, *Bully.*

Gray, Kes & Lee Wildish, *Leave Me Alone.*

Ludwig, Trudy, *Confessions of a Former Bully.*

Moss, Peggy & Dee Dee Tardif; Illus. Imre Geis, *Our Friendship Rules.*

Nickle, John, *The Ant Bully.*

O'Neill, Alexis; Illus. Laura Huliska-Beith, *The Recess Queen.*

Peters, Andrew F.; Illus. Anna Wadham, *The Ant and the Big Bad Billy Goat.*

Ross, Tony, *Is it Because?*

Wishinsky, Frieda; Illus. Kady MacDonald Denton, *You're Mean, Lily Jean.*

TEN CHAPTER BOOKS

Clements, Andrew, *Jake Drake: Bully Buster.* (Series)

Edwards, Michelle, *Stinky Stern Forever.*

Hogg, Gary, *Scrambled Eggs and Spider Legs.*

Howe, James; Illus. Melissa Sweet, *Pinky and Rex and the Bully.*

Maddox, Jake, *BMX Bully.*

Paterson, Katherine, *The Field of Dogs.*

Pilkey, Dav, *Captain Underpants and the Terrifying Return of Tippy Tinkletrousers.*

Richards, N.W., *How to Tame a Bully.*

Van Drannen, Wendelin, *Shredderman: Secret Identity.* (Series)

Wishinsky, Frieda, *So Long Stinky Queen.*

TEN NOVELS: GRADES 4-6

Blume, Judy, *Blubber*.

Buyea, Rob, *Because of Mr. Terupt*. (sequel: *Mr. Terupt Falls Again*)

Chan, Marty, *The Mystery of the Cyber Bully*.

Kerz, Anna, *Better Than Weird*.

Langan, Paul, *The Bully*.

Lekich, John, *The Losers' Club*.

Roy, James, *Max Quigley, Technically Not a Bully*.

Sachs, Marilyn, *Veronica Ganz*.

Spinelli, Jerry, *Loser*. (Also: *Wringer*)

Stolz, Mary, *The Bully of Barkham Street*.

TEN NOVELS: GRADES 7-9

Almond, David; Illus. Dave McKean, *The Savage*.

Fifty Cent, *Playground*.

Gardner, Graham, *Inventing Elliot*.

Howe, James, *The Misfits*.

Koss, Amy Goldman, *Poison Ivy: 3 bullies, 2 boyfriends, 1 trial*.

Palacio, R.J., *Wonder*.

Peters, Julie Anne, *Define "Normal"*.

Pignat, Caroline, *Egghead*.

Preller, James, *Bystander*.

Singer, Nicky, *Feather Boy*.

ANTHOLOGIES

Belleza, Rhoda (ed.), *Cornered: 14 stories of bullying and defiance*.

Booth, David (ed.), *Stand Tall* (Boldprint series)

Booth, David & Larry Swartz, *The Bully, The Bullied, The Bystander, The Brave*. (poetry)

Ellis, Deborah (ed.), *We Want You To Know*.

Gardner, Olivia, *Letters to a Bullied Girl: Message of healing and hope*.

Green, Joan & Kathy Lundy (eds.), *No Bullies Allowed*. (Boldprint series)

Hall, Megan Kelley & Carrie Jones, *Dear Bully: 70 Authors tell their stories*.

Porter, Helen Carmichael, *The Bully and Me: Stories that break the cycle of torment*.

Shapiro, Ouisie, *Bullying and Me: Schoolyard stories*.

Swartz, Larry & Kathy Broad (ed.), *Sticks and Stones*. (Boldprint series)

TEN REFERENCE BOOKS: AGES 10-16

Elliott, Michele, *Stop Bullying Handbook*.

Humans, Jackie; Illus. Nikki Lee, *15 Ways to Zap a Bully*.

Karres, Erika V. Shearin, *Mean Chicks, Clicks and Dirty Tricks*.

Ludwig, Trudy; Illus. Beth Adams, *Confessions of a Former Bully*.

Moss, Marissa, *Amelia's Bully Survival Guide*.

Proulx, Brenda Zosky (ed.), *The Courage to Change: A teen survival guide*.

Simmons, R., *Odd Girl Speaks Out*.

Slavens, Elaine: Illus. Brooke Kerrigan, *Bullying: Deal with it before push comes to shove*.

Stones, R., *Don't Pick On Me: How to handle bullying*.

Zerner, S., *It's Good 2B Good: Why it's not bad to be good*.

TEN FILMS AND DOCUMENTARIES: AGES 12+

Big Bully

Bully

Bully Dance

The Chorus (Les Choristes)

Cyberbully

Finding Kind

It's a Girl's World

Mean Girls

The Perks of Being a Wallflower

Terri

3. BULLYING WORDS

Writing in Role

When we write in role, we are invited to step into the shoes of others. As readers, we can understand the thoughts, feelings, and conflicts another person (fictional or real) might experience. Sometimes classroom drama lessons invite us to take on a role, or we can become a character in the books we have read.

ACTIVITY: BECOMING A STORY CHARACTER

After reading a picture book, poem, or novel that deals with a bully encounter, choose one of the following contexts for writing in role: the bully, a bystander, or someone who has been bullied. Or you can be someone who is not mentioned in the story but might know about the incident.

> Dear Recess Queen,
> How DID you get so bossy? Don't you want to have any friends? I guess you like being called Recess Queen, but I think you should stop doing such bad things. I hate being your victim. This cannot go on any longer. Even though I'm a teeny tiny kid, I'd like to give you a chance to CHANGE.
> Do you want to play jump rope with us?
> Yours,
> Katie Sue

You might

- Write a diary entry from a character's point of view in which he/she describes an incident and feelings about the incident.
- Write a letter of advice to a bully from someone who has been bullied. The sample in the box at left is written as a character in *The Recess Queen* by Alexis O'Neill.
- Write a letter to an advice columnist, describing the problem and articulating the feelings of the character. Then exchange letters with a partner and write back as the advice columnist, offering suggestions about ways to handle the situation.
- In role as a bully, write a letter of apology. In the letter, try to explain your behavior, offering reflections on why you think you behaved the way you did.
- Write a message for a Facebook wall for a person who has been bullied.
- Write a poem in the first-person (using "I") that describes how a character might feel.
- Write a letter as a parent of a bullied student. Letters can be written to school authorities, a bully's parent, or the bully.
- Prepare a newspaper or magazine report about a fictitious or real bullying incident.

Responding to Poetry

The Bully-Go-Round

by Larry Swartz

Round and round
The bully goes
Where she stops
Nobody knows.

Round and round
The bully goes by
Does no one hear
The trapped one's cry?

Round and round
The bully spins
A carousel ride
Where no one wins.

Bully goes up
Bully goes down
Bully goes round
And round and round.

The Darkness

by David Booth

It begins with a flash of light—
A warning.
Then the darkness floods my mind
And I begin the hunt.
Which young deer will be caught in my headlights?
Which rabbit snared?
Which fly trapped in my web?
It doesn't really matter;
It's the hunt that pulls me into the darkness
Until I am lost again.

ACTIVITY: TWO SIDES OF BULLYING

Work in groups of three or four to discuss:

- Which of these poems do you think has the most powerful impact?
- What message do you think the poet was offering?
- In what ways do these poems remind you of events you've experienced, heard about, or read about?

4. RESPONDING IN WRITING

Arts Approaches to Bullying

When exploring the bullying issue, we need to understand the behaviors of the bully, the bullied, and the bystander. The arts give us opportunities to reveal our inner thoughts and communicate our ideas to others through drawing, painting, moving, improvising, and presenting. By sharing ideas with others through artistic forms, we can work toward an understanding of how others might deal with challenging situations. The social, cognitive, physical, and emotional skills enriched through the arts can engender respect of others, an important value for dealing with bullying.

> ### Let's Talk About...the Arts
> - What are some challenges of dramatizing events that deal with bullying?
> - How is role-playing useful to build understanding of the bully, the bullied, and the bystander?
> - How can watching a play performance help us understand the lives of those who are bullied?
> - How does creating art help us deal with the thoughts and feelings around bullying incidents?
> - Do you think painting, drawing, and/or sculpting can help a young artist gain understanding of the bully, the bullied, and bystander?

ACTIVITY: LET'S DESIGN

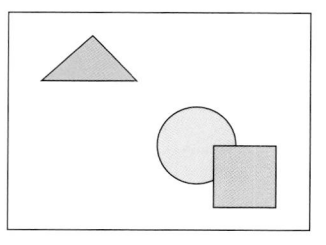

1. In this picture, which shape do you think is the bully? The bullied? The bystander? Discuss your answer with a partner or in a group of three. Be prepared to give reasons for your choices.
2. With cut-outs or by drawing a sketch, use geometric shapes (of similar or different sizes) to create your own design to represent the issue of bullying. Consider:
   - Will the shapes vary in size?
   - Will the shapes connect or be separated?
   - What colors would best represent mood and feeling?
3. Once it is completed, give your creation a title.

Extension

This art activity can be done in different media (paints, markers, construction paper, etc.), using the three geometric shapes as a foundation. Add lines of different lengths, thicknesses, and rhythms to create an art image.

1. Imagine that you have been asked to create an illustration for the cover of a publication titled "The Bully-Go-Round." Work independently to draw a sketch you would offer the publisher to consider. You do not have to include the title on your page. It is not necessary to include figures in this illustration; you might choose to prepare a design that represents the bullying issue.
2. As a follow up, share your drawings with others in the class. Discuss:
   - How many bullies were drawn as girls? How many boys?
   - How many illustrations did not show a bully?
   - What words have been included?
   - What is the story behind the illustration?

- What do you think each of the characters in the comic strip below might be saying? Fill the speech balloons for these characters. Work with a partner to compare dialogue.
- What might have happened before this scene? What might have happened after this scene? Working alone or with a partner, create two more panels, one showing what might have taken place before this moment and one that might take place after this moment. For each panel you can add speech balloons or thought bubbles.
- Create a graphic story that shows a bullying incident. Consider what characters say and think; if there is adult intervention; how the incident is resolved.

Exploring Poem Snippets

The following fragments, excerpted from poems about bullies, are suitable for art and drama responses.

"I cannot hide. It hurts inside."
"Don't get your pleasure from my pain."
"Life doesn't frighten me at all."
"I wish I hadn't joined in."
"Then one day he simply wasn't there anymore."
"Hey, you, c'mere!"
"Pain from the words has left its scar."
"I was in his power."
"You can't come into our street, our street, our street."
"We danced around him, sang our song."
"Every animal must choose between fight or flight."
"I don't know why I just stood by."
"I must be pretty clever."
"I bully the bully-bullies."
"Are they waiting for me?"
"We laughed. We whispered."
"Pain will cease, do not grieve."
"I was young and caught in the crowd."
"Please, please believe that I am sorry."
"Something inside shifts."

Let's Talk About…Reading Poems about Bullying

- Describe in one sentence what you think the poem is about.
- What is it about the poem that you particularly liked? Was puzzled by?
- What did the poem remind you of?
- What things in the poem did you see? hear? feel?
- What would you tell or ask the poet about the poem?
- Complete this statement: When I read the poem I wonder…

ACTIVITY: SNIPPETS AS INSPIRATION FOR THE VISUAL ARTS

Choose one of the snippets about bullies from the box to the left, or find your own. Using the technique of torn-paper collage (i.e., no scissors), create an illustration that represents this person's story, problem, or feelings.

- The art creation does not have to include figures or real objects in it; the paper can be arranged to serve as a metaphor for the inner thoughts and feelings of someone who is a bully or has been bullied.
- The snippet line of text can be written and included somewhere in the art image.

ACTIVITY: SNIPPETS FOR INTERPRETATION THROUGH CHORAL DRAMATIZATION

1. Working in groups, read aloud the snippets in the box on page 18. Each person, in turn, can read one snippet or more.
2. Repeat reading the snippets aloud, experimenting with different voices to bring meaning to the statements. How might a person say the lines to convey how he or she is feeling?
3. Repeat reading the snippets aloud. This time, add a gesture to show the character. How can this person communicate feelings through hand movement, facial expression, or posture?

Extension

Work with a group of five or six friends to present these lines of text as a choral dramatization. Each person in the group can be assigned one or more of the poem fragments. Consider the following issues of presentation:

- How will you begin your presentation?
- How will you add stillness or movement to join the snippets together?
- What physical shape will the group take as they present their lines?

ACTIVITY: SNIPPETS FOR IMPROVISATION THROUGH TABLEAUX AND ROLE PLAYING

1. Choose one poem snippet from the box on page 18. Decide if you think this line is told from the point of view of a bully, someone bullied, or a bystander. Why might someone say the line?
2. Work with a partner and create a still image showing two characters based on the snippet. Decide which character is going to say the line.
3. Discuss with your partner what might have happened to the character that would prompt her or him to have this thought. Improvise a scene to show a conversation that might have occurred in the past. The last line of dialogue in the scene can be the poem fragment.
4. Share your improvisation with others.

Extension

As a follow-up, write a short rhymed or free-verse poem that includes one of the poem fragments from the box on page 18. Add lines before and/or after the snippet to tell the story of someone who is caught in the bully-go-round.

5. BULLYING BY DESIGN

Drama Approaches to Bullying

Drama is one of the best ways to teach strategies to deal with a situation. The *what-if* context of imagined situations invites us to step inside the shoes of others and pretend that we are someone else, while considering our own beliefs and feelings. Through role-playing and working as if we were someone else, we can experience different points of views about a situation from an image, a story, or a script; this can help us understand those who are bullied, those who bully, and those who witness bullying. Body posture, gesture, voice, and utterances convey externally what is going on internally. The bullied can learn to protect, project, and be positive.

Working with an Image

ACTIVITY: TAKE COVER

1. Examine the illustration on the front cover of this book.
2. In groups of two or three, discuss:
   - What do you think each character in this image is thinking? Saying? Feeling?
   - Examine the two characters featured in the eyes. What do you think happened before this scene? What do you think might happen after this scene?
   - Do you think the face that is featured is a boy or a girl? How would the story be different if this is a girl character or a boy character?

ACTIVITY: LET'S IMPROVISE

Work in groups of three to bring the scene from the cover of this book to life.

- Create a one-minute improvisation that dramatizes what these characters might be saying to each other. Your improvisation should involve no physical contact.
- Repeat the activity, reversing roles. Improvise for two minutes.
- Reverse roles one more time. This time, role-play for three minutes.

ACTIVITY: GOING FORWARD IN TIME

The night after the incident, each character shown on the cover of this book has a conversation with an adult who has heard about the situation. What stories would each character tell? What advice would each adult offer?

- Work with a partner to rehearse an improvisation showing the conversation.
- Following the improvisation, dramatize the scene for an audience.

Working with Bullying Scenarios

Scenario #1: Samantha hates going on the school bus. The big girls shout rude things at her. She tells her mother, who says, "Ignore them." What should Samantha do?

Scenario #2: Ben moves to a new school. Everyone at the new school makes fun of the way he talks. Ben tells them to stop because they are hurting his feelings. They continue to mimic him. What should Ben do?

Scenario #3: Alex is being bullied at school because he is the shortest kid in class. His teacher doesn't know his classmates are making fun of him. Alex is afraid to tell the teacher what is happening. He thinks he will get in more trouble. What should Alex do?

Scenario #4: Lisa is being bullied by two girls in her class. They never hit her, but they demand things like money or food. Lisa agrees to give the two girls these things so she won't get hurt. What should Lisa do?

Scenario #5: Parvana is walking into the gym with her friend. She hears someone making a rude comment about the way her friend looks. Her friend doesn't hear the comment. What should Parvana do?

Scenario #6: Matthew tells Zack that he's been receiving rude e-mail messages. Zack knows who's been sending the messages but is told he'll get in trouble if he reports this person. What should Zack do?

ACTIVITY: IMPROVISING

1. Work in groups of three or four. Read the six scenarios. As a group, discuss your immediate responses.
2. Choose one of the scenarios and prepare a short improvisation that shows what might happen in the future to the person being bullied. Who might he or she talk to? How might the bullied person try to handle the situation? What things might he or she say and do to deal with the situation?
3. As a group, rehearse the improvisation to present to others.

ACTIVITY: WRITING AND PREPARING A SCRIPT

1. In small groups, write a short script that shows a day in the life of one of the characters from the scenarios. Consider:
   - How many characters will be in the scene?
   - Where will the action take place?
   - Will the scene describe a bullying incident or tell the story of how a character deals with the bullying incident?
2. Once your script is completed, rehearse and present the scenes to others.

Teacher Talk

Some recommended play scripts:

Brooks, Martha & Maureen Hunter, *I Met A Bully on a Hill*.
EFTO, *More Than A Play: A collection of nine short plays*.
Foon, Dennis, *Seesaw*.
MacLeod, Joan, *The Shape of a Girl*.
Twiddy, Brian and Yvonne Peacock, *Anti-Bullying Plays*.

Working with a Script

Setting: Outside the principal's office.

A: This can't be happening.

B: She can't be serious.

A: All I did was tap him on the shoulder after math class.

B: He pushed me.

A: He punched me.

B: And here I am. Again.

A: And now I'm in the principal's office?

B: The principal has made a mistake.

A: For sure she's made a mistake.

B: I'll sit here all day if I have to.

A: I don't want to make the first move.

B: The sky can turn purple.

A: I'll sleep here if I have to.

B: The grass can turn blue.

A: I'll go home and get my sleeping bag.

B: The trees can turn into giants.

A: I'll pretend I'm camping at school

B: But one thing for sure…

A & B: I'm NOT saying "Sorry."

—Script excerpt from *Tick Tock* by Allana Harkin (in *More Than a Play*)

Read the scene at left and discuss with a partner:

- Why did these two students get in trouble?
- How are the feelings of these two characters similar?
- Why are these two students not talking to each other?
- What do you think these two characters might say if they did choose to speak to each other?

ACTIVITY: REHEARSING

1. Work with a partner to read this script aloud, with each of you taking a role.
2. Repeat the activity, switching roles so that each of you has a chance to play both characters.
3. Work with your partner to direct this scene to be performed. Consider what directions you would give the actors. How will they say their lines? What gestures will they add? Will each character stand or sit?
4. Rehearse the scene and present it to another pair. Compare your different interpretations.

ACTIVITY: WRITING A SCRIPT

With your partner, continue the script: write the next 10 to 15 lines you think the two characters would say. Once your script is completed, rehearse and present the scene to another pair.

ACTIVITY: WRITING A MONOLOGUE

Imagine that you are one of the characters and you have been asked about the incident that sent you to the office. Write the story the way you think the character would tell it to a friend. Read your story aloud as a monologue.

Working with a PSA

A Public Service Announcement (PSA) is an advertisement broadcast on radio, TV, or the Internet for the public interest. PSAs are intended to change attitudes by raising awareness and educating the public about specific issues. Examples of PSAs on the topic of bullying can be viewed on YouTube, specifically those from Concerned Children's Advertisers; e.g. *Words Hurt, The Bully, Tell Someone*.

ACTIVITY: LOOKING AT PSAs

1. Work in a small group to investigate one or more PSAs. Prepare a report to share with others about each PSA. Include your thoughts on the following:
   - Who is represented in this PSA? Is everyone represented fairly and realistically?
   - With whom do you sympathize and why?
   - What points of view are missing? Do you think they should have been included?
   - How did the creators use sound, words and dialogue, camera angles, and/or music to make a statement?
   - Is the Public Service Announcement an effective format for informing the public about bullying? Why or why not?

2. Work in groups to prepare a PSA for others to view. Decisions need to be made about whose point of view will be represented. Facts and information that have been gathered about the bullying epidemic can be shared in the PSA to convince others to think—and act—on behalf of those caught on the bully-go-round.

Let's Talk About...Public Service Announcements

- How might PSAs be useful in preventing bullying?
- What are some of the essential features that have to be included to make a PSA effective?
- Think about some PSAs—on any topic—that you have found to be effective. Explain what it is about them that you think makes them work so well.
- Compare PSAs with anti-bullying posters (see page 26). How are each of these useful? In what ways does one medium work better than the other?

---

6. RESPONDING IN ROLE

How to Handle Bullying

There are no simple solutions in addressing bullying behaviors, but it is important to be taught the tools to use to stand up for our own rights while respecting the rights and needs of others, to handle conflicts without violence, and to act with integrity when confronted by all situations. Learning how to respect one another, value different opinions, share common experiences, and work toward a critical understanding of complex relationships and ideas is at least partly what school should be about.

Teacher Talk

Educators face no easy task in dealing with bullying. It is easy to point fingers, place blame, fortress our schools, mandate a bully-awareness week, stiffen penalties for bullying, or ignore the problem and hope it will go away. It is more challenging—and necessary—that we, in our professional roles, work with families and community members to create a safe harbor for our students.

Let's Talk About…the Bully

- Why do you think bullies behave the way they do?
- Look at the text in the next column. What do you think of Zerner's question to ask a bully?
- Look at the text in the next column. What do you think of Walsche's question to ask a bully?
- Does a bully have friends?

Understanding the Bully

Ignoring the problem or letting bullies off can suggest that using aggression or intimidation is a successful strategy for getting what you want. Having bullies understand their own actions is the first step in ending the terrible problem of bullying. Educator Sandra Zerner claims that bullies need to be asked this question:

"Would you punch yourself in the face?"

Zerner argues that those who are suffering in some way feel a need to hurt others. They are trying to displace their own pain onto someone else—and don't realize they're doing it.

To help bullies, we need to help them acknowledge their own pain. Neale Donald Walsche (Zerner, 2011) suggests that one way to do this would be to ask a very powerful question:

"What is hurting you so badly that you are willing to hurt others in order to heal your pain?"

ACTIVITY: WHY BULLY?

1. Working alone, write three answers to the question: *Why do some people bully?*
2. Exchange lists with a partner and compare your answers. Each partner can borrow one or two items from the other's list and add it to his/her own.
3. Working in groups of four, compare lists. As a group, compile a list of ten reasons why you think some people bully. Put a star or asterisk (*) beside each of the top three reasons.

Bullying encompasses a broad spectrum of behaviors, none of which are acceptable to caring citizens. Work in groups of five or six to brainstorm a list of bullying behaviors. Includes physical, verbal, and/or relationship behaviors.

Sample of Bullying Behaviors

Physical	Verbal	Relationship
damaging property	putting people down	acting rude
hitting	sarcasm	excluding
pushing	spreading rumors	ridiculing
finger-pointing	teasing	tormenting

Let's Talk About…Getting Help

- Do you agree with this advice that the Kids Help Phone offers as "Good News" to those who are being bullied?

  BULLYING CAN BE STOPPED
  HELP IS AVAILABLE
  YOU ARE NOT ALONE
  IT'S NOT YOUR FAULT

- Which of these four statements do you think would be most challenging to accept for someone who is being bullied?

Read the following scenario. What do you think the target could do to deal with the situation?

Lisa has recently arrived in a new school. Rachael makes fun of the clothes Lisa wears and, over time, starts calling her names. When Lisa was in the park, Rachael gathered her friends together and tried to force Lisa to hand over the new bracelet she got for her birthday.

Here are some choices that someone bullied has:

I yelled.	I fought back.	I stared him/her down.
I laughed.	I stalled for time.	I ran.
I said "no."	I told someone.	I invited him/her to my house.
I called for my friend(s).	I ignored it.	I cried.

Examine the chart above. In a small group, discuss:

- Which would be the most sensible thing for this target to do?
- Which would be the hardest?
- Which would be the easiest?
- What do you think you would do?

Extension

Write a letter of advice to the person who was bullied. What suggestions might you offer to best deal with the situation? Give reasons for your choices and give some evidence to validate your point of view.

Say Something

So you hear, see, or know about someone who has been bullied. What do you do? Where bullying is concerned, there is no such thing as an innocent bystander. If someone does nothing to stop a bullying situation, or does not tell or get help, then that person is part of the bullying. Statistics tell us that if someone intervenes within thirty seconds, a bullying situation can be stopped.

ACTIVITY: WHAT CAN YOU DO?

Anti-Bullying Strategies

A. Form a welcoming committee for new students.
B. Take part in the development of the school policy against school bullying.
C. Provide school staff with information about ongoing bullying.
D. Develop posters and brochures to publicize anti-bullying policies.
E. Look out for students who are having problems in their relationships; offer support.
F. Speak up in classrooms or at school assemblies.

In the box are six suggestions for actively participating in dealing with the bullying issue.

1. Work with three or four others to discuss the pros and cons of putting these strategies into action.
2. Rank the six suggestions in order from most effective to least effective.
3. Which of these strategies would you be most likely to help implement in your school?

The Anti-Bullying Poster

Visitors to most schools will spot a big, colorful placard outside the main office stating the anti-bullying policy of the school. Inside and outside classrooms, posters created by students reveal what they think about bullying and how the issue can be approached. We are certainly aware of the problem, reciting rules and the steps required to deal with such situations. With so much being done, the problem should be eliminated by now—unfortunately, it is not.

Let's Talk about...the Anti-Bullying Poster

- Are there posters displayed in your school that help build awareness of anti-bullying?
- Do you think a poster is an effective way to build awareness? To change behaviors?
- What information do you think should be included on a poster to have an impact on the students in your school?

ACTIVITY: POSTER DESIGN

Design a poster to publicize anti-bullying policies or to provide contact information for someone who might need assistance in dealing with the issue. Working alone or with a partner, create your anti-bullying poster to be displayed in the school environment. Consider:

- What image will be used to illustrate your message?
- What words will be included to catch someone's attention and to challenge them to confront the bullying issue?

Anti-Bullying in the Media

Films, documentaries, and TV shows can provide insights into those who are on (or watching) the merry-go-round of bullying (see list on page 13). We might experience strong reactions to these films but, through discussion in a safe environment, we can share our responses and come to understand how these stories can help us change our own lives.

For example, the film *Bully* offers case study experiences of kids, families, teachers, and administrators immersed in the challenges of giving courage to those who are bullied. This documentary, which began as a highly personal project for director Lee Hirsch and producer Cynthia Lowen, started a movement in the US and has become a rallying cry for victims of bullying who were shrouded in silence and shame. Response and discussion can help viewers uncover feelings and connections to a social issue that concerns all of us.

Teacher Talk

It is suggested that you preview the film *Bully* before sharing it with students, families, or the larger community. The book *Bully* by Lee Hirsch and Cynthia Lowen, an empowering companion to the film, provides an action plan for teachers, parents, and communities to combat the bullying crisis.

Let's Talk About...Bystanders

- Is it right to tell if it gets other people in trouble?
- How does doing nothing make a bystander part of the bullying?
- Besides telling an adult, what else might a bystander do?

Anti-Bullying Online

There are many websites to help young people, educators, and parents gain information about bullying.

ACTIVITY: REVIEWING A WEBSITE

Work in a small group to investigate one or more websites. Choose from the websites in the box below or find one on your own. Prepare a report to share with others about each website, highlighting the information someone can learn from it. Consider the best way that this information can be shared with others: oral report, written report, bulletin-board display, school website, etc. Include your thoughts on the following:

- Content: What powerful stories or information are shared in this website?
- Audience: Who might be interested in using this website?
- Effectiveness: How successful do you think this website is at providing information? What recommendations might you make for improving this website?

Barbara Coloroso www.kidsareworthit.com
Bullying Stories http://bullyinglte.wordpress.com
The Canadian Safe School Network http://canadiansafeschools.com
Cyberbullying www.cyberbullying.ca
Don't Laugh At Me www.dontlaugh.org
Public Safety Canada http://publicsafety.gc.ca
Kids Help Phone http://kidshelpphone.ca
Stand for the Silent http://standforthesilent.org
Stand Up 2 Bullying http://www.redcross.ca/article.asp?id=24700&tid=108
Start Empathy http://thebullyproject.startempathy.org

Supporting Student Awareness of Bullying

This outline suggests ten events that can be organized to promote bullying awareness in the school community. You can work alongside your students to consider which of these approaches can be implemented to further work toward an understanding of bullying.

1. **Buddy Reading**: Older students buddy with younger students and read a picture book to them. Buddy partners can discuss the themes and issues of the book: *What advice would you give the character? What would you do if you were in the bullying situation?* Buddies can work together on literacy and art projects that can be shared with others.

2. **Guide Book**: Students work independently or in small groups to prepare a guide book titled "How to Deal with Bullies." Each page in the booklet should offer a suggestion for dealing with the bullying issue; each page can be illustrated.

3. **Advertising Flyers**: Students prepare a flyer to build awareness of anti-bullying. A good flyer can be easily duplicated; should quickly capture the attention of an audience; uses visuals or captions. What message will someone get from looking at the flyer?

4. **Public Service Announcements**: A PSA is an advertisement broadcast on radio, TV, or the Internet that is intended to change public attitudes by raising awareness and educating the public about a specific issue. To prepare for creating a PSA, have students gather information about bullying from websites and print resources. Students can also view PSAs on the topic of bullying; e.g., *Words Hurt, The Bully, Tell Someone.* These can be used as models for creating their own.

5. **Movies**: There are many documentary and feature films that deal with the bullying issue. After watching a movie, have students discuss how it informed them about bullying. What questions did the movie raise? How true to life was the film? (See Ten Films and Documentaries list on page 13.)

6. **Drama Presentation**: Students prepare a drama collective that can be shown at an assembly. A number of drama strategies can be used for the presentation: tableau, monologue, improvisation, readers theatre, dance drama, song, choral dramatization, etc.

7. **Safe School Committee**: Some schools organize student-led committees to deal with problems and issues that arise day to day. Under the leadership of a school staff member, a group of older students can discuss ways to deal with bullying incidents, perhaps providing safe assistance to someone who is a bully, has been bullied, or has witnessed a bullying incident.

8. **Guest Speakers**: Police officers and other community members can be invited to raise issues about bullying incidents or to share stories about bullying incidents they have encountered.

9. **Website**: Create a class or school website to promote understanding of the bullying issue. Resources, as well as suggestions for dealing with tough issues, can be listed.

10. **Library of Resources**: Have students gather resources available from the classroom, the school library, and the community library that deal with the issue of bullying. The lists provided on pages 12–13 can support their investigation of resources. As recommended in Activity: Preparing an Annotated Bibliography on page 10, students can create an annotated list of suggested resources to help young children, older students, teachers, and parents access material relevant to the issue.

Professional Reading

Aronson, E. (2000) *Nobody Left to Hate: Teaching compassion after Columbine*. New York, NY: Holt.

Beane, A.L. (2005) *The Bully Free Classroom*. Minneapolis, MN: Free Spirit.

Brownlie, F. & J. King (2000) *Learning in Safe Schools*. Markham: ON: Pembroke.

Coloroso, B. (2002) *The Bully, The Bullied, The Bystander*. New York, NY: HarperCollins.

— (2005) *Just Because It's Not Wrong Doesn't Make it Right: From toddlers to teens, teaching kids to think and act ethically*. Toronto, ON: Viking.

— (2007) *Extraordinary Evil: A brief history of genocide*. Toronto, ON: Viking.

Galey, P. (2004) *Keep Cool! Strategies for managing anger at school*. Markham, ON: Pembroke.

Garbarino, J. (2002) *And Words Can Hurt Forever: How to protect adolescents from bullying, harassment and emotional violence*. New York, NY: Simon & Schuster.

Henkin, R. (2005) *Confronting Bullying: Literacy as a tool for character education*. Portsmouth, NH: Heinemann.

Hinduja S. & J. W. Patchin (2008) *Bullying Beyond the Schoolyard: Preventing and responding to Cyberbullying*. New York, NY: Corwin.

Hirsch, L., C. Lowen, & D. Santorelli (2012) *Bully: An action plan for teachers, parents and communities to combat the bullying crisis*. New York, NY: Weinstein.

Jacobs, T.E. (2010) *Teen Cyberbullying Investigated: Where do your rights end and consequences begin*. Minneapolis, MN: Free Spirit.

Klein, J. (2012) *The Bully Society*. New York, NY: New York University Press.

Lundy, K.G. (2004) *Teaching Fairly in an Unfair World*. Markham, ON: Pembroke.

Lundy, K.G & L. Swartz (2011) *Creating Caring Classrooms*. Markham, ON: Pembroke

McQuade, S.C. et al. (2009) *Cyber-Bullying: Protecting kids and adults from online bullies*. Santa Barbara, CA: Praeger.

Parsons, L. (2005) *Bullied Teacher: Bullied Student*. Markham, ON: Pembroke.

Pepler, D. & W. Craig (2000) "Making a Difference in Bullying" at http://www.melissainstitute.org/documents/MakingADifference.pdf

Rigby, K. (2001) *Stop the Bullying: A handbook for teachers*. Markham, ON: Pembroke.

Shariff, S. (2009) *Confronting Cyber-Bullying: What schools need to know to control misconduct and avoid legal consequences*. Cambridge, MA: Cambridge University Press.

Simmons, R. (2002) *Odd Girl Out: The hidden culture of aggression in girls*. Orlando, FL: Harcourt.

Simmonds, J. (2003) *Seeing Red: An anger management and peacemaking curriculum for kids*. Minneapolis, MN: New Society.

Stones, R. (1993) *Don't Pick On Me: How to handle bullying*. Markham, ON: Pembroke.

Swartz, L. (ed) (2004) The Bully Issue of *Orbit*, OISE/UT Vol. 34, No. 2.

Swartz, L. & D. Nyman (2010) *Drama Schemes, Themes & Dreams*. Markham, ON: Pembroke.

Willard, N.E. (2007) *Cyber-Safe Kids, Cyber-Safe Teens: Helping young people learn to use the internet safely and responsibly*. San Francisco, CA: Jossey-Bass.

Wiseman, R. (2002) *Queen Bees & Wannabes*. New York, NY: Three Rivers Press.

Index

Dedication:

To my OISE candidates, past and present

Larry Swartz has explored literature-based learning with students and teachers for more than 30 years in North America, England, New Zealand, and China. As a classroom teacher, consultant, and instructor with OISE/University of Toronto, he has inspired colleagues and children alike to learn in new and exciting ways. Larry is a well-known speaker and workshop leader and the author of numerous practical books for teachers, including *Creating Caring Classrooms*; *Drama Schemes, Themes & Dreams*; *The Novel Experience*; *The Picture Book Experience*; *The Poetry Experience*; and *Good Books Matter*.

© **2013 Pembroke Publishers**
538 Hood Road
Markham, Ontario, Canada L3R 3K9
www.pembrokepublishers.com

Distributed in the U.S. by Stenhouse Publishers
480 Congress Street
Portland, ME 04101
www.stenhouse.com

We acknowledge the financial support of the Government of Canada through the Canada Book Fund (CBF) for our publishing activities.

We acknowledge the assistance of the Government of Ontario through the Ontario Media Development Corporation's Ontario Book Initiative.

FSC
www.fsc.org
MIX
Paper from
responsible sources
FSC® C017783

Library and Archives Canada Cataloguing in Publication

Swartz, Larry
    Bully-go-round : a handbook of literacy and arts strategies for promoting bully awareness in the classroom / Larry Swartz.

Includes index.
Also issued in electronic format.
ISBN 978-1-55138-285-2

    1. Bullying—Prevention—Study and teaching. 2. Bullying in schools—Prevention. 3. Language arts—Correlation with content subjects. I. Title.

LB3013.3.S93 2013   371.5'8   C2012-907594-9

eBook format ISBN 978-1-55138-851-9

Editor: Kat Mototsune
Cover Design: John Zehethofer
Typesetting: Jay Tee Graphics Ltd.

Printed and bound in Canada
9 8 7 6 5 4 3 2 1

In our society, where emerging technologies unite and divide us in new ways, bullying is reaching epidemic proportions. *The Bully-Go-Round* shows teachers and students powerful and positive ways to connect, react, and respond to stories and information that lead to a better understanding of the issues around bullying.

The book illustrates the complexity of the bullying cycle and explores the role of those involved: the bully, the bullied, and the bystander. More than 35 activities offer interesting ways to respond through talk, in writing, in art, and in role to challenging bullying issues. From bullying in the digital world and bullying statistics to responding in writing and exploring anti-bullying in all media, the book offers innovative ways that teachers can support students toward confronting and stopping the cycle of bullying. Activities include

- studying relevant advertisements and websites
- responding to poetry about bullying
- designing artwork, graphic stories, and posters about bullying
- creating tableaux and choral dramatizations
- improvising, writing, and preparing scripts

This timely book lists the best books and other media, grouped by genre and age level, to use with students in Grades 1 to 12.

Discussion prompts and tips for teachers on creating safer classrooms complement this valuable resource for students, teachers, and the school community.

Pembroke Publishers Limited
538 Hood Road
Markham, ON L3R 3K9 Canada
www.pembrokepublishers.com

ISBN 978-1-55138-285-2

Front Cover Photos: Danish Kahan, 1MoreCreative / Getty Images